Worries

Paul Christelis

Illustrated by Ximena Jeria

W
FRANKLIN WATTS
LONDON • SYDNEY

Questions
and Feelings
About ...

Franklin Watts
First published in Great Britain in 2018 by The Watts Publishing Group

Copyright © The Watts Publishing Group, 2018

All rights reserved.

Editor: Melanie Palmer
Design: Lisa Peacock
Author: Paul Christelis

ISBN: 978 1 4451 6395 6 (Hbk)
ISBN: 978 1 4451 6396 3 (Pbk)

Printed in Great Britain by Bell and Bain Ltd, Glasgow

FSC
www.fsc.org
MIX
Paper from
responsible sources
FSC® C104740

Franklin Watts
An imprint of
Hachette Children's Group
Part of The Watts Publishing Group
Carmelite House
50 Victoria Embankment
London EC4Y 0DZ

An Hachette UK Company
www.hachette.co.uk

www.franklinwatts.co.uk

Worries

Questions and Feelings About ...

Have you ever worried about something? Maybe you've been invited to a party and you're worried that you won't know anyone else. Or perhaps someone you love is ill and you're concerned about what might happen to them.

We all have worries from time to time.
Parents, friends and teachers can all worry.
It's a normal part of life.

What do you worry about?

When worries fill our heads, they can make us feel anxious. Anxiety can make us feel unwell.

We might feel all wobbly inside,
or our hearts might beat faster.
Maybe our bellies ache or
we don't feel like eating.

*How do you
feel when you
are worried?*

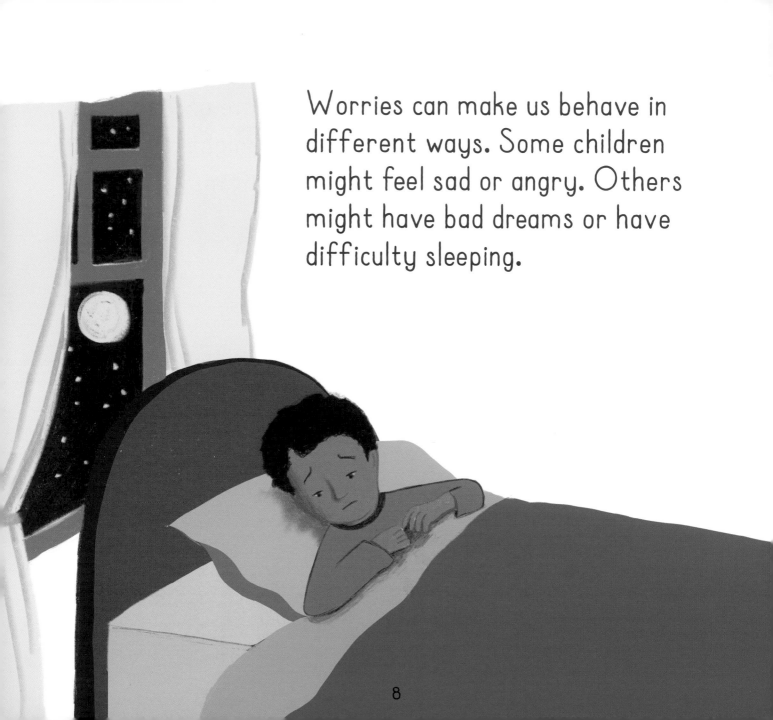

Worries can make us behave in different ways. Some children might feel sad or angry. Others might have bad dreams or have difficulty sleeping.

You might find it difficult to concentrate or feel scared to try new things. Or you might not feel like going to school or spending time away from your loved ones.

Sometimes, worrying can be useful because it tells us that something is wrong and that we need to get help. If your friend got hurt in the playground you would worry for them and take them to the school nurse, or call a teacher.

But worrying can also be unhelpful.
This happens when we imagine
bad things happening to us
even though there is
nothing wrong.

Sometime we may worry about bad things happening by asking ourselves 'What if' questions, such as 'what if I fell out of a tree? or 'what if my dog was ill?'

What questions would you ask yourself?

Worries are nothing more than unfriendly thoughts. The more we think them, the more anxious they can make us feel.

But there is good news! Even though these thoughts feel real, they are not.

They are only thoughts. You can't hold a thought in your hand, or see the shape of a thought.

Try it for yourself: think about a pink elephant. Can you see one in your mind? That pink elephant is only a thought, you can't really touch it, or smell it, can you?

It's the same with worries. Even though the worries are not real things, our bodies still feel anxious when we think them. Our bodies believe that the worries are real!

What can you do to make yourself feel better when you are worrying? Luckily, there are many things that can help.

You can choose to place your attention on something that is happening now rather than get lost in worries about the future. A good place to start is to focus on your breathing.

See if you can feel the air moving into your nose as you breathe in, and out of your nose as you breathe out. Notice how each breath is different.

You can also notice what's going on around you. If you are outdoors, you might feel the warm sun on your skin or see the colours and shapes of plants and trees.

Listening to sounds can be very calming:
birds tweeting, a breeze blowing, or
music playing. See how many different
sounds you can notice.

After taking in sights and sounds
for a few minutes, you will probably
notice that the
anxiety and the
worries are not so
loud anymore.

*What do you hear
when you are outside?*

It also helps to write your worries down, or draw them. Once you have done this, fold up the paper and place it in a Worry Box (you could use a shoe box, or tissue box).

Place the Worry Box on a shelf or in a cupboard. You can open the box at the end of the week and empty the worries. You might realise that they aren't worries anymore.

Sometimes, all we need to do when we are feeling worried about something, is to talk to someone: our parents, caregivers, brothers, sisters, friends – anyone we trust.
Even our pets!

Sharing our worries helps us to move the anxious feelings out of our bodies. It's like opening a window in a stuffy room: fresh air flows in and everyone feels better.

It's also helpful to remember that very often things seem worse in our imaginations than they really are ...

... and we are often a lot braver and more able than we think!

Notes for parents and teachers

As a parent, teacher or guardian the most important thing you can offer a worrying child is your time and attention. Listen to their concerns. Let them know that it's normal to have worries, that everyone experiences these at times. Once you have provided a safe and non-judgemental space for the child to express his or her concerns, there are effective ways to help soothe them. Here are a few suggestions:

Let your child know that the worrying thoughts they are thinking are simply thoughts. Thoughts are like traffic: they come and go; sometimes there are many, and sometimes not. It can be unpleasant to be stuck in traffic, but sooner or later the road will clear and the noise of the traffic will fade. Worries are similar: thinking them can be noisy and unpleasant, but if we are patient we notice that they don't last.

Worrying thoughts usually show up in the body as unpleasant sensations. Identifying and naming these sensations in a calm and kind manner is a powerful way of helping your child to deal with the unpleasantness without 'catastrophising' or amplifying the worry. Diverting attention from the worry to the sensation of breathing can calm the anxiety associated with worrying. It's easy to do and only takes a few moments.

Having enough sleep, a healthy, balanced daily diet and regular exercise will promote physical and mental wellbeing, and help equip children to better manage worry and anxiety.

Classroom, group or home activities

1. Discuss how worries can be dealt with via a 'Worry Lorry'. Ask children to make their own 'Worry Lorry' by writing their worries on strips of paper that can be placed inside. The lorry carries these worries away, and at the end of the day, the papers are removed and recycled.

2. Ask children to imagine any unpleasant sensations they feel as weather patterns in the body. Invite children to share what they notice: 'Tell me where you're feeling the worry weather right now' (often, this is in the chest, belly, throat or head). Then, ask them to describe the feelings to you, as if they were weather presenters on television describing the latest weather. As with the Worry Lorry, they begin to notice that these feelings are nothing more than feelings, and that, like the weather, they are always changing.

3. One effective breath exercise for keeping calm is 7-11 breathing. Breathe in through the nose to the count of 7, pause, and then breathe out through the nose to the count of 11 (repeat this a few times). This enables the out-breath to be longer than the in-breath, which allows the parasympathetic nervous system (PSN) to become activated, responsible for soothing the stress response in the body.

Further Information

Books

How Are You Feeling Today? by Molly Potter and Sarah Jennings
(Featherstone Education, 2014)

Exploring Emotions: A Mindfulness Guide to Exploring Emotions (Mindful Me)
by Paul Christelis and Elisa Paganelli (Wayland, 2018)

The Huge Bag of Worries by Virginia Ironside and Frank Rodgers
(Hodder Children's, 2011)

Websites

anxietyuk.org.uk (support for adults and children)

childline.org.uk (includes a section on anxiety, stress and panic)

mind.org.uk (national mental health charity)

youngminds.org.uk (mental health issues for children)

Every effort has been made by the Publishers to ensure that the websites
in this book are suitable for children, that they are of the highest educational
value, and that they contain no inappropriate or offensive material. However,
because of the nature of the Internet, it is impossible to guarantee that the
contents of these sites will not be altered. We strongly advise that Internet
access is supervised by a responsible adult.